SEASONS OF LIFE

A BOOK OF HAIKU
BY
MEL GOLDBERG

Rolemi Publishers

Also by Mel Goldberg

Poetry:
The Cyclic Path, 1990
Sedona Poems, 2001
A Few Berries Shaken From the Tree (haiku), 2010
If We Survive, 2011

Prose:
Choices, (A Novel), 2003 reprinted 2011
A Cold Killing (short stories), 2010

ISBN 13: 9780982734544

A special thanks to my life partner Bev Kephart without whom none of this would be possible

ACKNOWLEDGEMENTS

Several of the haiku in this book were previously published
in the following periodicals:

Paper Wasp (Australia)

Shamrock (Ireland)

Heron's Nest (USA)

Acorn (USA)

To every thing there is a season,

and a time to every purpose under the heaven:

a time to be born and a time to die,

a time to weep and a time to laugh,

a time to mourn and a time to dance,

a time to seek and a time to lose,

a time to keep silence and a time to speak,

a time to love and a time to hate.

From Ecclesiastes 3:2-8

The universe is an immense symphony with each member contributing its unique sound in harmony with all other members. The seasons are part of the order. Poetry is one expression of the great harmonic order in the universe and haiku is the synthesis of that expression.

Enoch Tan

A TIME
TO BE BORN

April beggar's cup
tissued bottom muffles sound
silent charity

another glass of wine
spring moon hides his face   behind the
mountain

stone streets glow
in wet reflected light
May moon beckons

after March floods
he preaches absolution
to cleanse his soul

springtime
leaves and I in the forest
for the first time

copper canyon
the Tarahumara boy
runs the way of the clouds

dried spring daffodils
in Wordsworth's book of poems
pressed memories

♦♦♦♦♦

in the quiet pond
a frog sees
sky and clouds

♦♦♦♦♦

hamantaschen pastries
filled with prune and poppy seeds
I taste my childhood

elk tracks in snow
soon melt and disappear
words on white paper

we gaze heavenward
but fail to see blossoms
trampled underfoot

green pines, white aspens
distant worlds revealed
in the deer's eyes

early May morning
the full moon still trapped
by the lake

in the first bite
of a freshly-picked peach
the end of ignorance

it is spring again
the old man walks his dog
alone in silence

spring morning
heron fishes near the shore
clouds hide the sun

morning coffee
sun dappled through spring leaves
rising steam

my string stretches fully
as spring wind raises my kite
I also would be free

rainy season
mountain trail up the mountain
lost in clouds

crisp spring morning
the scent of pine
quickens my step

after the scorching spring
the cicada chorus
sings for rain

my path starts
at the edge of the lake
full April moon

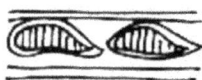

the sound of shofar
sonorous waking notes
ancient memories

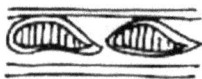

early spring morning
the mirror reflects sad eyes
the river flows

to the universe
I send an invitation
with forever stamps

soft spring rain
rivulets of clarity
on my dusty window

on the blackened edge
of my pink eraser
yesterday's words

late April days
smell of roads I must travel
urging in the blood

childhood reminders
on the wooden door frame
penciled growth marks

Passover seder
my father calls my infant son
by my name

blue moon butterfly
perched on a garden leaf
eyes looking at me

spring campfire
red faces
dancing shadows

spring morning mist
the spider web
gathers diamonds

A TIME
TO SEEK

August rainstorm
green guayabos
litter my patio

a walk on the beach
surging waves erase footprints
sommer sea

in empty shells
gathered on the beach
I whisper, "Yes"

walking the morning trail
my face breaks web connections
summer solstice

night of shooting stars
the deaf child looks and wonders
if they make a noise

a murder of crows
sleep on the scarcrow's shoulders
warm summer night

a violin solo
from the house next door
summer solstice

July evening
owl hoots from the oak tree
my loneliness echoed

freshly cut grass
the snail marks his silver trail
across the yard

lightning flashes
trees and mountains
in black and white

three cups of saki
I swim the diamond river
milky way

the tallest pine
reflection distorted
water wind wave

I stuff my pillow
with spring and summer lives
I have outgrown

Peru dolphin
on the Maroñon River
a flash of pink

English garden
a ladyslipper dares to grow
in the footpath

a train rumbles past
childhood memories caught
in the whistle

cormorants bob
with herons on dark water
reflecting moon

July blue moon
reflected on the still lake
one canoe

the roses
I neglected in the spring
still produce summer blooms

white summer clouds
floating on the lake
mountain pelicans

walking on the beach
I pretend to be
a younger man

a glass of summer wine
a shadow passes
in front of the moon

ocean pelicans
glide inches above water
motionless wings

rainy season
the mountain trail disappears
sea of white clouds

summer buzzing
chicharras sing in the trees
prayers for rain

hiking the mountain trail
I stop to notice
flowering weeds

agave glows blue
on the steep mountainside
afternoon sun

through an open window
the full moon enters my room
cold silent thief

windy summer day
trousers on the clothes line
dance a frantic jig

on the pantry shelf
I find an unlabeled tin
maybe summer peaches

my father stays with me
the way a horse's flowing maner
in flowing manes keeps summer

to greet the new day
my eyes also open
daisies

butterflies flutter
wings beating haphazardly
flower dreams

A TIME
TO LOSE

rockets announce the holiday
my little dog
cuts her walk short

rainy season past
the green hillside
wears autumn brown

summer in the meadow
pine trees huddle
in paragraphs

sunset reflected
in windows of the house
I no longer own

my Mexican village
swallowed by the shadow
of the mountain

on the road again
where will today take me
a leaf on the stream

even when no wind blows
autumn maple leaves still fall
hunter's moon

October camping trip
the smell of wood smoke
lingers in my clothes

the blind beggar
listens for the sound of coins
in an empty cup

grandmother's house
the scent of old breath
lingers in the kitchen

I put another coin
in the parking meter
to buy more time

border fence
the moon slips through
between the boards

a fall visit home
someone mentions your name
my eyes fill with tears

autumn sunset
on my patio table
an empty wine bottle

all my yesterdays
gathered within me
autumn heart

August sunset
the red cliffs reflect
ancient memories

Yom Kippur
I think of all the things
I failed to do

in the pond
a frog sees sky and clouds
beneath him

on the horizon
of all my yesterdays
a single sail

sunset
the homeless man
unfolds his bed

dia de los muertos
flowers and music
in the panteon

funeral libation
the wine weighs heavy
in our glasses

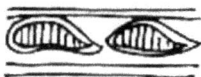

autumn evening
the deer come at sunset
to harvest the field

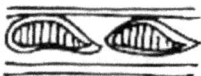

ocean pelicans
glide effortlessly above waves
water dreams

passover seder
ancient slavery story
I too was freed

in the wings of birds
there are metaphors
autumn equinox

day of atonement
the undescribable joy
of being hungry

into the stone soup
I drop another pebble
end of summer

my once youthful face
reflected in the mirror
textured by time

grief fills the pockets
of my autumn trousers
golden maple leaves

monarch butterflies
fill my apricot tree
I close my door

battlefield in autumn
even the air
is propaganda

dried daffodils
in Wordsworth's book
pressed memories

A TIME
TO DIE

winter fire
the sound
of popping pine

a cloud of white doves
take to the air as one
winter breath

I express my thoughts
to the expanding universe
starry winter night

a good friend's obituary
the whoosh of wind
through the trees

as evening settles
we make plans for tomorrow
as if we'd be here

sunny day
I see snow-capped mountains
winter comes

black and white photo
winter at Manzanar camp
everyone is smiling

grandmother's house
the smell of mint on my fingers
no one left to remember

memory of the moon
lingers in my gin and tonic
after you have gone

abandoned building
cracked windows reflect pain
silent snow

hair red as rust
memory of my father
breathes within me

winter moon
plays peek-a-boo
through bare branches

crab tree blossoms sing
morning glories tell stories
snowflakes lift my heart

the old dog
still cases cats in his sleep
winter dreams

winter tree
a single leaf in the wind
memory

once I sang the earth
now I cannot remember
autumn loneliness

winter evening
the ever vigilant rabbit
hears the owl

across the cold land
the frozen lakes are motionless
clear water beneath the ice

my body grows old
withers and wrinkles
cherry blossoms in winter

freshly fallen snow
I follow the tracks of birds
searching for seeds

I tell part
of my story
snow falls

funeral home
she straightens his tie
for the last time

Sante Fe opera house
an aging tenor smiles
yellow poster

New Year's eve
we forgive each other
for old mistakes

she awakens
to his callused hand
the sound of snow

rain at your funeral
mud on my shoes
mud on my shoes

cold December night
the frozen surface of the lake
stares back at the moon

on the patio wall
ristas sway back and forth
winter wind

a month after your death
I am unable to delete
your phone number

I look in the mirror
my father's face
looks back at me

winter creeps
into the canyons
silent fog

sea glass smoothed by waves
crevices in my face
time's alteration

in the barren field
wind-swept dust reminds us
forgotten rain